Sharp Pencil
Joe Pascoe

First published April 2022 by Reading Sideways Press

20 Tennyson Street, Richmond, VIC, 3121, Australia
readingsidewayspress.com
readingsidewayspress@gmail.com

This book is copyright. The copyright of the original text belongs to Joe Pascoe. Except for private study, research, criticism or reviews, as permitted under the Copyright Act, no part of this book may be reproduced, stored in a retrieval system or transmitted in any form or by any means without prior written permission. Enquiries should be made to the publisher.

Typeset in Avara and Caudex

National Library of Australia
Cataloguing-in-publication data is available
at http://catalogue.nla.gov.au

ISBN 978-0-6454725-0-9
Designed by Amarawati Ayuningtyas
Proofreading by Michele Fuller

READING SIDEWAYS PRESS   RSP

Urban Imaginaries

for Lyndel

Acknowledgements

My profound gratitude goes to Andy Fuller and Nuraini Juliastuti for producing and publishing my poetry, from half a world away in Leiden. They share the limelight with my family – Lyndel, Eve and John – who knowingly accept the eccentricities of life with a poet. One friend amongst many, Norman Rosenblatt, dispels my concerns with his response 'Still making mistakes!' when I ask him how he is going.

I am very thankful to Professor Sean Redmond for his generous foreword, written in Melbourne's dark, quiet winter of 2020. My thanks also go to artist Mark Cain and fellow poet Robert Nelson for their encouragement in reading so many poems on the way to this book being realised. The artworks by Sam Golding have joyously lifted their pages and given the whole volume a special air. And I am also thankful to Adam Bos and the NDIS for supporting creativity.

Foreword

The sandy beaches of the Otago Peninsula in New Zealand can sometimes be found coloured with a red hue, leaving the coastline looking like it is an open wound that naturally bleeds. This phenomenon is created by the squat lobster, otherwise known as *munida gregaria*, whose settling instinct means it clings to surfaces even if in so-doing they perish. The squat lobster settles in sand at high tide and refusing to let go at lowtide, ebbs away into cardinal oblivion. This is a reproduction instinct rendered a death vow: they settle to spawn and die trying.

There is very much the life and death instinct coursing through the arteries and veins of the collected poems found in *Sharp Pencil*. The idea of *Sharp Pencil* is that it offers keen observations about life. It has a loose story arc that references the act of drawing. Section headings called Lines, Shade and so on to Last pages, place the reader within a poetic world.

Couplets jive with tercets and quatrains. Melancholy heats the memories that are revealed or confessed and a sense of loss and longing caresses the tips of its metaphors and the warm stomach of its everyday mode of undress. At the same time, *Sharp Pencil's* nostalgia for the past brightly steps us into the present and calls forth hopefulness and chants out the metres of love. These are *settling* poems, refusing to let go of the five o'clock shadows they fall upon, while drawing back the net cardinal curtains to let the new day in.

In *Old Crocodile,* for example, an imagined long day of reflection allows the narrator to reminisce about the carefree freedoms their youth had offered them and the limitations of their aging present. The wish for a new haircut and a few dollars in their pocket is contrasted with the contemporaneous feeling of not wanting to be alone and the superbly ironized conceit of the wealth of prescribed health. Half rhymes coupled with irregular patterning, alliterations with staccato phrasing, accelerate and decelerate the temporality of the poem, embodying its past-present tense, putting it on edge. The poem ages with its narrator and its last lines recall Dylan Thomas's *Do not Go Gentle into that Good Night* when it powerfully concludes with:

> Leave the bitterness alone
> No arrogance needed anymore
> Curb the rage though keep the anger
> It adds colour
> To the beige.

Like many of the poems in the collection there is a concentration on the ordinary and the minutiae of domestic life. Everyday objects are acutely tuned with reminiscentia, as carriers of affective memories. A flowering cactus connects us to the memory of grandpa eating pink ice cream in the garden. A swim in the ocean embraces the hands of a nondisclosed grief.

Pegging washing on a clothes line recalls a friendship and the mood lines that runs through yellows and blues. Ritualised events take centre stage: a Christmas beach walk, a holiday overseas, a dance, a visit to a sculpture park.

In many ways the poems offer an oblique audio-gaze on domesticity: as if in the homes we visit we are hearing infrasound or our point of view is peripherally positioned. *Sharp Pencil* shows us what is underneath the familycarpet, what is left behind in the kitchen sink.

The collection of poems also enables us to better understand what holds and collapses in the fields of remembering and forgetting. Poems grasp at completeness as they recognise how frail memorial narratives are. In *Rusting*, the narrator struggles to remember the name and function of the metal object they are restoring: all that is left in the memory box is the set of micro-actions, and the senses of the textures and materials that are been rubbed. This sensory journey back to 'underneath the house' also reveals something about our relationship to existence itself. One where the world comes to us not fully formed, nor solely or inevitably shaped by language but one where our experiences take flight, uncoupling us from representation. As Maurice Merleau-Ponty writes, 'we know not through our intellect but through our experience'. When I read *Rusting* I don't search for the 'name' of the object that cannot be remembered but revel in the glint of the metal, the blackened fingers in tectonic motion, and the underneath and undisclosed spaces that reside in our homes, rusting like memory. As the poem, *Painted Words*, also reminds us,

> Sometimes the words disappear
> In love and elsewhere
> The other life we lead
> Needing no language
> Nurture it too
> Colours in your mind

> Which blend with others
> To a picture make
> Without any fears

Sharp Pencil is pocketed by sadness. The narrator laments time passing but also the caves of loss brought on by the death of one's parents. In the sublime *So Simple*, the anguish brought about by losing one's mother is captured through a fractured lens where clocks, bed sheets, tea and biscuits, and the 'I am sorry for your loss' platitudes of nurses knit together to reveal the withering hours that come with mortal grief. The lines 'Death is hard/It stiffens the face' remains an imprint long after it has been read. There is a hauntology that hangs its ghostly coat over many of the poems in this collection: the persistence return of the past, and a critical nostalgia for what has gone and for lost futures. This haunting is carried into the literary and artistic allusions that a number of the poems draw upon, including Stendhal, the 19th century French novelist; Francis Bacon, the 20th Century expressionist painter; Fellini, the Italian neo-realist filmmaker; and Stefan Szonyi, a Hungarian ceramic artist. Together they become a carnival of lost souls, savaging the stanzas, staging the melancholy, filling the past-present with their terrible beauties. In *Scared Pope*, for example, we find the 'streaky violet of the curtains' are the very drapes that sin and falling befall.

The collection is also one of resistance and rebellion: in *Scattered* the narrator asks us to 'Draw in some clouds/ Sunshine' to resist the routines and the order of the everyday. Very often it is the use of colours or the notion of colour itself that stands in relief to the monochrome, monotone and the metronome. Fern Gully green. Gold sparkles. Carrot and squash. Pink and funny. Lush green dope. Orange fringe. Yellow acrylic. These pallets wash the stanzas with a colliding naturalism, a new materialism, that hopefully refuses the 'beige'. In these fecund poems humour and satire also finds their way in. Acerbic wit always attaches itself to the looking backwards and its associated melancholia. For example, in the wonderfully funny *On a rock* we find the narrator's daughter lampoon the poems that in turn lampoon them: 'How about this for a book title' she is asked. 'On a rock' is the reply, 'uttered to her iPhone'.

Poetry humanises people and it turns language inside out, opening up the world to new impressions, sensations, revelations. Poetry's canvass belongs to everyperson but too often is situated within high art contexts and is defined and delineated in limited ways. Presented as a higher art form it can alienate the young and exclude those with limited cultural capital. My interest in school was sparked by poetry: my way wardness channelled and recuperated after hearing and reading the delicious works of Seamus Heaney and W.H. Auden. I have taught poems and poets that have caught the imagination of working class kids and allowed or enabled them to find rhyme and reason.

This is what *Sharp Pencil* reaches for and achieves: set largely within a suburban Australia, in the kitchens, gardens, and public spaces that the narrator dwells in or returns to, we find everyday life beautifully caressed and assessed, with objects, people and memories rising up in all their oblique majesty.

The poems patiently sit on the sands of a pristine beach, next to the squat lobster, as the tide ebbs and flows. It would be easy for poem and lobster to just let go: to not settle, to give up on life. This they cannot do.

Sean Redmond, May 31 2020

Sean Redmond is Professor Screen and Design, School of Communication and Creative Arts, Deakin University.

Contents

I **Lines**

Draw	22
Sharp pencil	23
Sparrows in the lane	25
Pinball machine	26
Selling papers	27
Magpie day	29
Merry-go-round	31
Teenage puzzle	33
First cigarette	36
Yeah	37
Headlights	38
Airport	40
Poetry	42

II Shade

Wattles by the creek	45
Lunch with John	46
Young birds	49
Poesy of weeds	50
Favourite plants and reasons	51
Father and daughter	53
Boys in the tree	54
Finders keepers	55
Father and son	56
Balsa wood	57
Sailing away	58
Sailing with our father	59
Museum boy	60
Mr White Pants	62
I paid off the mortgage	64
For her home	65
Happy	67
Words	68
Poem soup	70
Bordertown bakery	71

III Colours

Scared Pope	75
Green sash	77
Praying mantis' secret	79
Blow fly	80
Uniqlo T-Shirt	81
Gallery Break-up	82
Nanna's quilt	83
Roof tops	84
Painted words	85
Christmas times	88
New trumpet	89
Joyful bauble	90

IV Broken Grey Lead

Bombed	93
Drunken focus	94
2020	95
Zoom funeral	97
Half day	99
Groove	101
Polite Melbourne	103
Together	104
Scattered	107
Old crocodile	108
War's end	110
Amnesia	114
Stendhal says goodbye	115

V Pencil Shavings

Old warbler	120
Ava	121
The trees are talking to me	122
Sherbrooke Forest	123
Paddock	124
Brave	125
Night time radio	126
Astra concert in real time	128
Didge	130

VI Dots

Outside the alphabet	133
Homage to metrical poetry	134
Dice	135
David	136
Ivanhoe maple tree	137
Kim	139
On a rock	142
Hard to title	143
Rusting	145
Circle	146
Torquay sunrise	147
Little fishes	149

VII Last Pages

Last dream	153
So simple	155
Innocent snow	158
Burnt forest	160
Three old men	161
Columbarium	163
Bits of time	166

Epilogue

Great Mountain	169
Unring that bell song	171

LINES

Magpie

Draw

Sharp pencil
Look around and see
Scrape and shade.

Sharp pencil
for Sam Golding

Sharp pencil
Honed to a perfect cone
Breathe on the lead
Exiting any shavings

Hold it like a pen
Or flat to shade
Easily done
Mind and body

Draw as you walk
Imagine scrawling out white clouds
Or lovingly compose a street
Add wiggly birds
Diminishing in flightIt's easy

Flip the page
It might be a cat, ambitious
I have a friend who can do this
Outline, clever strokes
Textures and mood
Sam Golding

Look at the lead
Warming and rounding
Less pressure
More pressure
Light and dark

Draw more, learn more
Stones and water
The day itself
People in life
Life within trees
Sunlight through the leaves

Joe Pascoe

Sharpen again
Less pointy, more forgiving
Kinder to your friends
As the black lead ages
As your pencil shortens
And the beautiful drawings pile up.

Sparrows in the lane

for Drs Beverley and Alan Larwill

Sparrows in the lane
Quite a few
I love them
All those fluttering greys
Looking sharp
They never threaten and will sing
Just happy it seems
Talking as we skim past
Every one busy

Sparrows in the lane
Picking and pecking
Away from the cats
The colour of the Richmond sky
They fly off as a fly past
Free with no worries
We all live here
Down the lane
Known only to us

Sparrows
You are little like me
You don't miss anything
You can't be caught
You have had some food
And look cool
Kinda like me
Little sparrows in a group

Usually one is alone
Quick and fast to take off
Hop, hop and away
I want to be like you
Pretty birds in the grey sky.

Pinball machine

Slot machine physics
Hamburger with the lot
Marlboro on fire
Clack
Boing
Clack
Twitch the switch
Ping the paddles
Crack, double score
Bite the burger
Refresh with coke
All good
Glass and lights
Tilt and lean
My friends are keen
We did so well
Time spinning on
Twenty cents only
Our colours flashing
Flicking fingers

Smoking hot!

Selling papers

Traffic lights
Mullcahey's pub
Missy Low milk bar
Us
Guitar shop
Butcher cheat
Chinese man with fine ham
Cameron's paper shop
Fruit Palace
Chemist with a pretty girl
Hairdresser with top cigarette lighters
Up to the next hotel
On to the early tofu shop
Vlado's steaks opposite, that's funny
Dry cleaners, Pharmacist, Jewellers

I sold Heralds
I built my own paper round
Keep going
Mr Frango shoe repairs, a great man
Richmond Hill Cellars
Lennox Street corner
Some kid threw a stone at me, big deal
Another kid wanted my money, no way
Sold the last few papers
To cars and people
Twenty cents, keep the change
Thank you!

I could pick them, the tippers
How they reached for the money
I flicked out the paper and folded it
Cupping the same hand for the money
Smooth, really smooth, I practiced

Joe Pascoe

My small hand blackened by the print
Remembering not to wipe my face
Great with the change, quick
Proffer it, don't fake a fumble
'Keep it'
Thanks, said warmly
I learnt that.

Magpie day
vale John Wischer

Cold fingers, cold knees
Purple bruises, pink freeze
Magpies swooping, protecting their young
No questions asked, I've gotta run

Oh, they have the finest warble
Caramel with cherry notes
Black and white feathers
Liquorish and Ghost Gum tones

They make friends in the afternoon
Take the front lawn
Like knights on a chess board
Zig zagging, jumping left and right
Warbling, ready for a fight!

Paired for life
Dad and Mum and their young
I see them solo or in twos, swinging through
They will make an appointment, if you choose
Little crumbs, away from the house
Stand there and throw out bread
Maybe say hello and nod your head

I don't think they feel the cold
Birds are flying dinosaurs, seeking prey
So sharp and smart, see them dance
Twitching their firm bodies around
Hard to predict on the ground

You are allowed to rhyme some popular poems
As everybody knows, you are being kind
Sentences that flow into the mind
Even today, when my legs are cold

Trying to recall memories of old

Were they that different?
How did you wake?
Groggy or excited, both?
That was my youth

Longing for long pants
Gloves, scarf and a woolly beanie
Pockets in my jacket, hands rammed deep
Stuff that magpies don't keep
Their round nests have no doors
Beautiful twigs and found bark
Coracles camouflaged, in the dark

You will never hold one
But you can converse, discourse
Their talking answering your warm whistles
Be patient and kind
Float thoughts from your mind
Land

Some people warble just like magpies
I don't mean to be mean
But they can attack unseen
Like kids with cold legs running home for tea
That's not how I want to be
Magpies, you and me, enjoy being free.

Merry-go-round

Violin streak
Moving notes
So high
Like a fly

It stops
Bends to a bass
Joins in

Whistles through
Lemon sounding
Don't touch me
Return away
To your reflection

Piano chords
Ruffle harmlessly
Giving the violin
Somewhere to play

Timpani
Where are you?
Trapped
Not doing a percussive thing
Offset the tinkle please

Give some form
To the twirling sound
Merry-go-round

Notes floating up and down
In a carousal of song
On golden poles
Dipping and riding
Giddily around

Joe Pascoe

Never let it stop
Fairground man
Your tattoos and smoke
Make it real!

Teenage puzzle

There was little to say
It could have gone either way
Mystery or explanation
I thought
Words tangled together
Sometimes it's better not to speak
People wear out
They don't want to hear more
You have to guess why
Walking is the way to go
Walking not talking
It's the step
Your legs floating then landing
Like breathing
Oxygen in, carbon out
Maybe there is no knowledge
Just special vibes
Radiating or not
People alone with their shoes
Clothing their thoughts
I like this mood
I might chase it down
See what's inside
It's a mixture
Past and future
Standing balanced
Standing on the see-saw
Juggling emotions
Feeling for perfect balance
Left and right
Fore and aft
Jump down on the chips
Sprint away
To home, toward the warmth

Capturing the dawning moment
Sensing a realisation
Before its definition, its' flash
Drawing you like a magnet
Toward others
Away from home
But I like to think
As well as play
As life falls apart, walls cracking
Ceiling ripping, lights sparking bad
Watch it smoking
Those flames are dangerous
I can't tell you what to do
Just what I did
I ran
Around the corner
Hide
Take a look
Filter away
Playground and home
Gone and gone
That's how life works
Rough changes every time
Find a friend or two
That's what you do
Thread through the chaos
Share if you can
But zip up your pockets
Don't let them trick you
I don't know when my life changed
It was unstructured
Mess floating still
Like a flood
I headed for purpose
Work and security
Forms stiffened

I kept it clean
Made it look fine
Mine
Time has turned its handle
Around and around
Notes tinkling out
Last one remembered
The next one plucked
I'm back on that see-saw
Enjoying the balancing act
It's a cool thing to do
Saving up my thoughts
To write a better future.

First cigarette

The first smoke
Nice and early
With coffee
A tiny sip
Then crack the pack
Tap one out
Coordinate the action
Pack back in the jacket
Light the fag
Little but mouthful drag
Blow out
Pucker the lips
And another sip
Swirling smoke and sweet coffee
On our way for another day
Not a lot more to say
Fairly neat
Ash somewhere
Drink
Everything going
Lungs and stomach
Cheering the brain
All set and dressed
Keys in my pocket
Other stuff
Toward the door
Car cold to touch
Settle in
Butt out.

Yeah

Five toes clenched
Spray down my back
Total fear and love
That's how
I surf
Mixing fate and hope
Screaming and laughing
Not feeling wet
The shore is coming
Ready to dump

Sitting in the sand
Enjoying a juice
Staying lean, getting ready for you

Stretching out
Feeling your lips
It's warm now
Waiting to see what you do
We smile our way through

Properly dark
Night has fallen
It's good here, low
I really feel close
The stars
Reaching blue
Like you
So far away
Never to return
One fuck
Fading away
Bit sad, so true.

Headlights

for Wayne Giles

Headlights
Ahead and behind
Overtaking on my mind

Slipping along
Fog providing cover
Police nowhere around
But I'm happy
Nudging 115 without much sound
A few seconds for a life
Is not my game

Puccini or John Lennon
Standing by me
It's a curve gliding down

Car lights flashing in the trees
Keep neat as I please

I let it lift to 125 then squeeze
Back from the breeze
It's early morning
The sun is stretching
A fair way to go

Petrol just trickling through
Four cylinders beating true
Heater mostly on
Leaving the headlights floating too
Road pitch even
Tyres all tight 140
It's a dream
My machine
More cars coming to play

Going each way
Nearing a town
Gotta slow down
Drop to 105 and cancel the beam
Look local
Know what I mean?
Flip down a gear
Foot off
Hit 60, before I stop.

Airport

Taker of time
Taking off
Taking on
In between you breathe
Barely
Body in a slump
Decked
No country
Spinning without feeling
The earth rotates beneath you
Chasing the curve
Or sliding off

Off in London
30 pounds city train
Stinking and heavy
The gravity of culture
Museum of manners
This library book returns
Read once in the bright sun
Page corners turned at will
No more

The footpaths are the same
Same but more so
Endless brits in step
My weary gait accepts
It's part of the trip

We flew over the setting sun
To return 'home', to England
Weaker now
With age and stale hope
Gone the antipodean light, free leaps and odd twists.
Instead the Roman conquest

I walk
Suitcase rolling
Reading the signs
They say go back
To Jack
Be as good as your master
Says Jack
In the land with an outback.

Poetry

Opaque, a feeling only goes so far
Then it returns back to you
Telling, letting, you know that's all
You see a truth

It's held in a moment
A meeting point
Desire and beauty
Luminous beyond the text
That's the feeling
It stops the mind

And there it is, quiet, dark, poetry.

SHADE

Magnolia

Wattles by the creek

for Lyndel Wischer

Flags of colour
Almost no perfume
But fresh in the mind
Winter's flowering wattles

Stretching up the creek
Vista splotched with yellow
Leaning over the bike path
A cathedral in the Darebin parklands

Encouraging us to walk
Reminding us in an unsentimental way
Spring and summer
Green and dark bark
Singing along the way

The Darebin Creek is flowing well
Rocks just appearing
Water shearing over
Muddy banks soaking through

Birds and bees
Healthy fronds of fluffy flowers
The wattle trees arch over
Returning each year

Huge in impact
Waking the Australian bush
The start of a new year
Not January but August
Golden Wattle
Waving us through
Turning our conversation to love
Love for place

Love for people, with grace.

Joe Pascoe

Lunch with John

A poem in honour of Florentino's

You order the beef cheek
It arrives with mashed potato
Firm white cloud
Red wine and blood
Staining its cliffs

So soft, the cheek
Decadent yet logical
Not something to chew
Easy on the jaw
As our conversation stiffens
Such sangfroid, so Proustian
Our thoughts dissect the situation

A war had started in Ukraine
I ordered the fettucine
Its tangle a metaphor
For what, Europe?
Well, it could be
But it's a tangle
A menu option
A detached search for perfection
Of which it was and wasn't

Our restaurant is a renaissance painting
We act together within its frame
The agreed norms
Its prices even
Waiters weave through as though from another century
They ensure our participation
A play from the menu

In time we discuss most everything
We are good at this
It's an agreed dance
News, history, culture
A gentle joke here and there
Lunch as it should be
And no office or shop needing us

Age is kind to us
Two violins in the corner
Timbers reflecting the light
Strings still taut
That's us, on a good day!

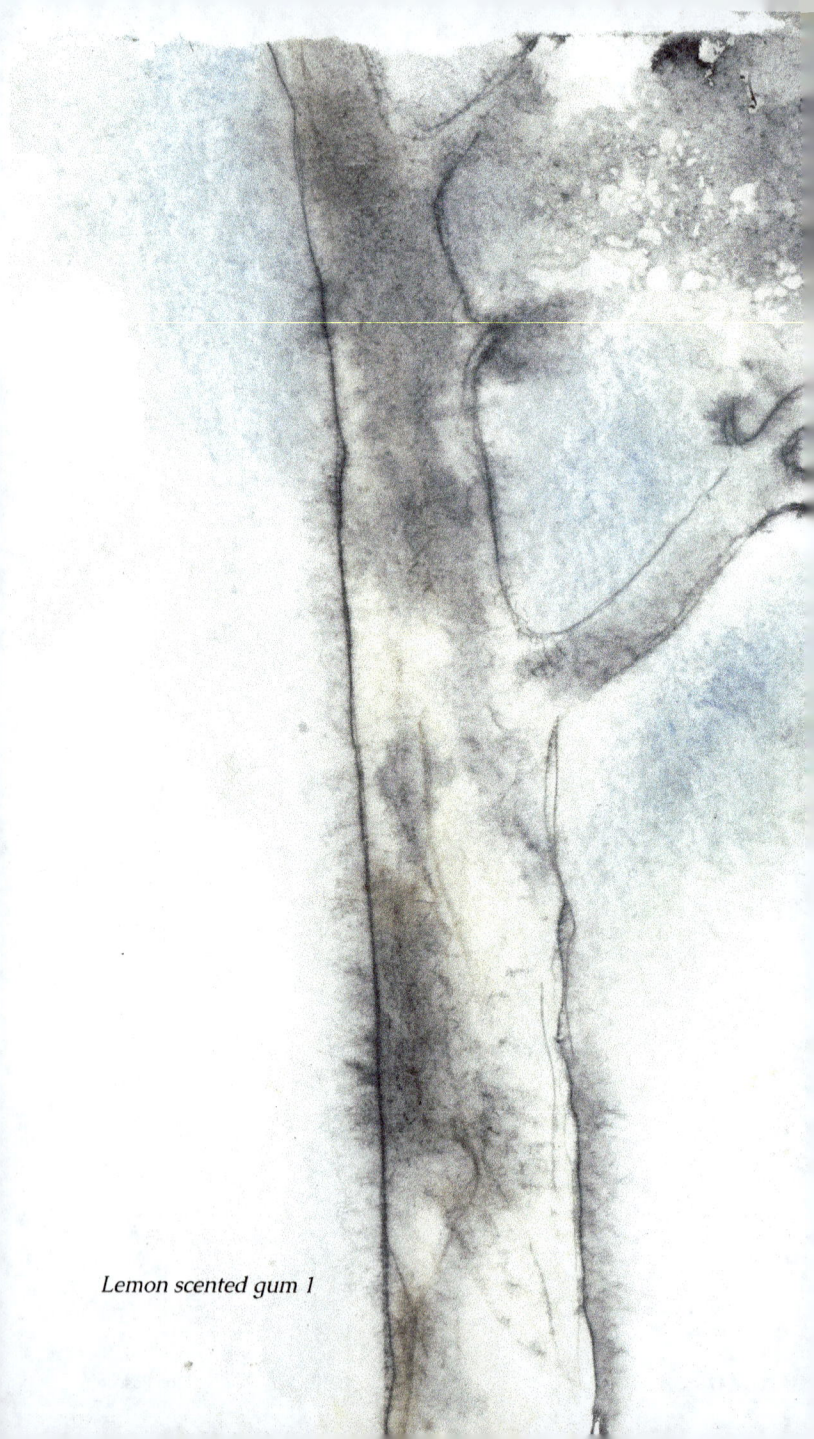

Lemon scented gum 1

Young birds

Brothers and sisters
In perfect eggshells
Prettiest pale blue with inky spots
Or off white with freckles
Heaven and land
Together in the nest
Round and woven
Like wind
A portend of their lives to come.

Poesy of weeds

for Mother

Long grass
Picked in twos and threes
Fold in a weak bark strip
Some leaves
Let your fingers add
Any sorts of flowers
To make a poesy of weeds

Run inside
There is a vase in the cupboard
White op-shop, gilded and fancy
Twist up the stems
And push them in
Turn on the tap
To the brim
The job is done
Put it on the table
For mum.

Favourite plants and reasons

Sweet Williams
Small curving mounds with many white flowers
Arranged in rows
In formal gardens of childhood
Perhaps near a monument
Guiding my steps with joy

Bracken fern, seen in green gullies
A strong pattern
Making my legs cool
Brushing us, protecting us
As we hiked through
On course

Hedges I like too
More than I'll admit
Their solid patinas
Controlling space
Making the footpaths pleasant

Moss I'm fond of
It can be accidental or deliberate
Found in private contemplation
An enjoyable scale
Moist

Let's hear it for the colossal Bunya Bunya
Tough tall ancient
Very small very regular
Sharp leaves in their thousands
Forming a canopy that defies mostly everything

Jonquil flowers
Yellow, white and orange
A pleasant, easy bunch Perched in a vase
Or growing in nice soil
In grandma's Seaford garden

There are the amazing ones as well
Gymea Lily sending its red crown
Metres in the air
Proudly
Popular are the native grasses
Best seen in secret groups in Gippsland
Enjoying the rains
Incredibly healthy
Special but not inviting attention

I like particular trees
It might be a river gum
Full of character
So thick it predates white fella
Watching the Darebin Parklands

Bush land, botanical gardens
Flower pots with red geraniums
Windy paddocks
Holding on to bent melaleucas
Forming furrows in the sky

We all like wattles
Giving hope in winter
We plant sprays of brown and olive
Picked with some colour
In our gardens
To mark our place
In the wide landscape
Of our lives.

Father and daughter

for Eve Pascoe

Father and daughter
My daughter is very alive
But just as brittle as a ceramic
Do not harden your daughter
Nurture her, support her always
Listen and try not to yell
Men should not be feared
Believe in her
Realise that the day is long
Night and day
Do not let your daughter walk away
Always be by her side
Somehow, with love.

Boys in the tree

Bikes on the grass
Standing up easy, somehow leaning
Shiny bikes, not expensive but nice
Spokes glistening, real and full size
Two fresh voices from the tree
Young boys talking
Thrilled to be up there
Safe and excited
Gathered by the muscular branches
Proud and ancient in Sparks Reserve
But it was the eagerness that got me
Talking to each other
Two metres up
Bonding in adventure, legs dangling
Well-spoken and happy
Not breaking a taboo
Enjoying the sunshine

Maybe a lifelong friendship
Born in that moment
An hour of play, confident
Ride to the tree, their tree
Climb its thick trunk
Unbroken by the years
You and me, in that gum tree
Away from the world
Looking out, feeling free
Surveying the land
It felt like flying
Bikes safe below
Down we go
And ride on home
Our secret, silently made
It's ok to be like this
Those fresh voices
Floating from the tree.

Finders keepers

Twenty cent feather
Thick rubber band
When you find something
It's yours
In contract with fate
No one else knows
The freedom to find
To realise and take
From the ground
Is settled by gravity
The greatest law of all
That's why.

Father and son

for John Pascoe

On being a father
You have to know your son
As he changes, as he grows
A baritone or tenor
He will need to be heard
So listen to him
He should likely hear you
Just say it once
Mostly with an easy way
Talk with him, hear his advice
It's given with pride
Let him know your feelings
Be logical too
Persuade if it's important
But join in the fun
With your son.

Balsa wood

Balsa wood
Flat and sticks
Make a plane
Paper and glue
Knife slices through

Planes that don't fly
Or boats that lean
But balsa wood
To you
I can never be mean.

Sailing away

Puff
Blow
My boat floats
Modest but real
Ice-cream sticks
Paper sail

Toy soldier on board
Brave little man
Green and armed
Rifle in his hand

We sail on
Across the great sea
As soap bubbles bloom
I examine its course
First to the centre
We crab along the side

It goes well
I add a wave
It ripples through
My man topples off
Time to go
And place my raft above the trough.

Sailing with our father

for Bobby

We sail away from the shore
Out from the beach
In sight but lost
Its people meaning less
Life on the boat grows
As important as any destination
Cigarette and sherry
Feet wet by spray
Relaxed
There was no end
Each trip linked
Punctuated by the clunk of docking
Walking on hard earth
Easily caught by others
Like fish out of water
Boat hoisted and tidied
Its dreams stowed
The sky smiles
We're calmly home.

Museum boy

Teach yourself books
Pleasant diagrams, wind surfer
For on the sand
How to play table tennis
Improve your bowling
Spin, fast, flat
Charming

In my hands and in my mind
For on the street
Sailing on a lake
Snuck a look
How to box

Clear drawings, short notes
Beautiful work
But kissing a girl?
That needed a tutor

My library visits
Adventures
Rare books and maps
State Library of Victoria
Museums of the mind
Get out what you find

Medieval armour, wonderful weapons
Pistols, you know
Shown on an angle, jaunty curator
Clocks, horology, proud
I walked on

You could almost run
Room to room
Fill your mind
Satisfy yourself

Put it in order
Look at the stage coaches
Miniature trains, like grandpa's
But no Pascoe on the label

I was good then
Did not steal, quiet
Washed clean, shoes and socks
Not distorted yet By events unseen

The strength of it all
Collections, dates, countries
So very special
Objects in cabinets
People in suits

Swimming in knowledge
Things to learn
Learn to remember
Series of art works
Spot the gaps
Judge the paintings
Examine the etchings
Understand the frames
The lighting, the hang
Old school now

Buildings
Fat entrances, skinny halls
Around and around you go
Pause at the book shop
Marvel at the texts
The prices, believed
Outside to the street
Smile at those you meet
Eyes wider
Footsteps grander
For a block or more.

Mr White Pants

Art gallery director
Art gallery director
Show me a sign
Is my work divine?

You stand
You float
In a room
So white

I can't touch you
Nothing can
There you are
Here I am

I can't touch you
Nothing can
There you are
Here I am

You smile
Me too
Please put my painting on the wall
I promise to crawl

Not so
Not necessary
Hate you or love you
Your painting says it all

Be free
Be cool
Don't be blue
It doesn't suit you
The emperor has no clothes

Art gallery director
Gallery director!
Don't let your pants fall down.

I paid off the mortgage

Riding a good mood
For over a week
I mostly paid off the mortgage
It made my wife happy
And the kids think
I became useful
And I agree

I paid off the mortgage
Australian magic come true
Money blew in
When mum flew away
I paid off the mortgage
And feel settled today

It's our family
That's what
I cherish
Tensions gone away
Who would have thought?
Such an easy thing to say

Returning to normal
Keeping sane
I can go shopping
Build again

Letting it flow
Rising to a new plateau
I want this simple feeling
To never go.

For her home

Sharp needle
Poking through, piercing the tension
Dragging its cotton thread
Up with a taut pop
Diving back down, puckering along
As memories close the gap

Sewing does this
Talking to textiles
Starting a conversation
Moving lips softly
As the cloth talks back

Cloth bought and cut
Purchased and carried home
Laid out and chalked
With a flat piece of white stone
Marking with care
My daughter's curtains

She moved out last week
Her first flat
I love her dearly
And live a little through her
As all mother's do
Imagining her buying fruit
Making happy friends
Safe, on her path
Let it have flowers

A small private curtain
Just for the kitchen window
I picked an easy pattern
Floral design with floating cameos

Joe Pascoe

Breadsticks and vino
Softly merging dreams and reminders
Wipe the surfaces clean
Enjoy your cooking, my chef

I cannot live her life
It can't be
But I can be there
With quick hands
As I sew

For you.

Happy
for Dr Leonie Griffiths

Happy is yellow
Favouring an orange fringe
Arcing over you
Bursting
Batting away the blues
Greening new thoughts
Contributing, helping, flying
You see nothing else
It's you

Washing your clothes
Glorious suds
To be pegged to the line
In windy sunshine
Ready for folding and care
Picked and chosen across the days ahead
Redistributing the soft glow

Fresh and clean
Simple joy
Your inside showing through
To those that love you.

Words

for Tasma Wischer

I like my words
Well, on the page
In my mind, too jumpy
On the radio, in song
Over the counter
In a shop
On the phone

They march in emails
Ants of the mind
Carrying a heavy load In lines, busy and dark
Words, words, marching

Make paintings with them
Try to add wind and sun
Crops too
To eat
Eating words!

Great words
Like please and thanks
In tune, in place
Open and done
Strings in time
Linking thoughts and actions

There are a lot of them
Children that grow
Playing first, then working
Scientific words, all sorts
Up then down
Cars over horses
Petrol over hay
Driver for rider

Road for track
Meanings moving
Sounds shift
Poems remember

I hear my family
Familiar and so alive

Doors opening, words in rooms
I listen for their rhymes
And silent mimes
Dancing syllables, colouring in
A painting for my wall
Hanging in my head
A gallery for me to see
Without prices, treasure for free.

Poem soup

Umm not sure
The cupboard is dark
A packet jiggles
By itself
I catch it

Find a pot
Sauté onion in olive oil
Sprinkle in letters
And watery sentences
Spicy paragraphs
Three
Awkward to stir

Hmmm salt and half rhymes
Vowels for body
Any veggies from the fridge
Chop them first
Always stir

It's too thick
Too rich and thick
Needs a weak concept
Pepper and punctuation
Beans into the mix

Aarrhh it's working
Lots of consonants bubbling up
Simmer and let the story come
Steady and slow down
It's that kind of poem
Let it sit a while
Serve with bread
Might need some parmesan .

Bordertown bakery

for the Fuller family

Lamingtons snowing in the shop
Featured with easy charm
Singing to me
Through the clean sloping glass

I glance along
Back and forth
Pendulum stopping
Custard or fruit slice
Stops on the hedgehog

Where did they get their names?
Were their journeys so different?
Able to last a whole day
Then sleep the night
Waking at dawn

Bakery light on
Making bread from four
Powdered like ghosts
Working in the heat
Darkness yet to lift
Good bread for homes
Pies for all

Country bakery standing still
Year after year
A carnival of cakes
Cars stop, door dings
Shop sign determined to say hello
In that proud small town
Between Melbourne and Adelaide
One Sunday morning
Taking away your loneliness

Joe Pascoe

Drive on
Out of town
Down that highway
Away from Bordertown.

3. COLOURS

Butcher Bird 2

Scared Pope

I am the odd blue
Oily and present
A layer on the surface
Waiting for Francis Bacon
He paints at night
Drenched with whisky
Cigarette and lover hanging off him
Yet, he wants...
He wants a pope to appear
In expensive gauze

At midnight
In the early morning
This rich man
Can do as he pleases

I am wet
And smell of smoke and linseed
Mixing some hell with laughter

Night longed for day
Francis is tired now
Some food with the sweet music
Sleep comes and the canvas slacks
Bacon will return
To play with purple and grey

His pope will come
Summoned
Not knowing why
He is alive in this way
Streaky violet for the curtains
As our souls fry

Why Francis Bacon why?
He screams at your punishment
In our canvas
Stretched out bare
No religion to spare
Compelled to fall forever
Paying in pain
No scales of justice

No redemption, no receipt
Only infinity's grace
To which you must now pray
Smudged in grey.

Green sash

for Stephen Pascoe

Ned Kelly
Waiting
Last hour
Setting like concrete
Getting ready to drop
Like a rock

You rode free
Taking it on
The plains
Hills and creeks
Fires and horses
Men and love
They really wanted to break you
You missed seeing your mother
You wore iron
Because that is what you were
They shot at your legs
You kept on
Knowing the lead would bring you down

The rope feels good
Top quality
As good as can be woven
Better than you could afford
You did not piss yourself
I don't need a hood!

Fast drop
Crack
Body probably bucked then slacked
They all stood there
Measuring themselves against you
Each man composed

Drooping a little
Some scurried into place
Doing their tasks
Into a coffin
Death mask, three or four
History is not sure

It's glib to say
But
It's true
Your history began
With those last words
Thrown by you

We visited Greta
A rough paddock of a cemetery
Cracked paths with weeds
The simplest layout
Not a lot of people there
Hot and windy bare
No frippery
I went and had a piss
On a gum tree
Aiming for a spot outside the cemetery
I felt ashamed
Having felt your presence
From over a fence

Buried deep without a sound.

Praying mantis' secret

Praying mantis
At my front door
On the glass
Green as grass, a few bits stick out
Some legs, four

The dance
Left front, back right
Back left, front right
Very cool

Why, why?
Or
Yhw, yhw!
Inside out and around
Standing its ground

Looking fit, trim
Earnest and mysterious
I breathe ever so gently
We only have a minute together

I look away
Ease my head back, still there
Mesmerized
I seem to forget
Then, gone.

Blow fly

Watching the blow fly, fly
Circle and dive
Buzz and maybe splutter

Off again
Welcome to summer, my friend
Black wavy line
Right to left
Gone quiet now

Always seems ready to die
Carking on the window sill
Other black dots
Legs upside down
A final droning sound

I hear another one
A relative or friend
Impervious to me, just too lazy
We three

Are they watching?
5,000 eyes
Is that true?
Bloody blow fly
I'm waiting for you!

Uniqlo T-Shirt

in homage to Clive James

Uniqlo Hokkaido t-shirt of my dreams
Blue all around all the seams
Same waves rampart
Traveling to my heart
You were mine from the $15 start

In union keeping me going
In my terrific t-shirt
I am wearing in hope
Not really for power I am weakish today
Pale in a way

Let's hope the t-shirt helps
I like it too much
It's impossible design
Straightening my hippie spine
Those times were so fluid
Our soft jeans were embroidered
My pockets bulged with lush green dope

But no more
That's for sure
Officer put away that gun
I was just having fun
In my Uniqlo Hokkaido t-shirt.

Joe Pascoe

Gallery break-up

White, white blue and white
Red blocks red blocks red
In a brown and gold frame
On the white wall
Soft leather shoes, soft leather in you
We look on
Thinking about the time
How long does it take?
We go on

Silver cross silver cross silver
A golden ball swings by
Bye bye
Our time is over
You and I are going nowhere
It's over baby blue
I don't get you
Or maybe I do

And it's happening
With you with you with
Out out out
I go
Blue blue no
It's coming down
This curtain this
Spluttering to a stop
No relationship
An aching pain instead.

Joe Pascoe

Nanna's quilt

People settle into their patterns
Me too
We mainly all do
Our blanket
Decorated with memories
Moment is seen and sewn in
Worn close or worn loose
Discarded at times
Dropped when snoozing
In the old folks home
Or drawn close when cold
More patches
Shared and lost
Like scarves and brollies
Left in cafes
Found on trains
Between in and on
Folded
Spread on a bed
In colour.

Roof tops

Richmond skyline
Roof tops angling around
Wind flurries, hot sound
Which way to look
Past or present
Both containing a future

Happy people in a beer garden
Stretched out
Warmed on the concrete
Watching Molly
In his green triangle
Kind of free
Our Meldrum

Hints abound
Trains bound past
Swan Street piazza
Below our roof garden
Swelled by art
We cheer

Lennox Street looking posh
Flavours of South Yarra
Better than SY
Never diminished
Always its history
Holding me tight.

Painted words

for Deborah Halpern

Always the difference
Between the word and the thing
Fantastic
Not really
Just part of life
It's not the adjective's fault
When we should sing
Or write a poem
I think

At a certain time
In mid-childhood
The words come
We read in words
And hear them in our brain
But when we speak
The magic remains

Run a line of words
A horizon line formed
In that we pray
I'm getting excited now
Feeling exalted with thoughts
Attach them to a place
A type of find
That stands in for a fact
To hear the church bell ring

Better the metaphor
Than the drab
Sentence of a street
To wander without really touching
With your feet
Sometimes the words disappear

In love and elsewhere
The other life we lead
Needing no language
Nurture it too
Colours in your mind
Which blend with others
To a picture make

Without any fears
Paint in words
Rejoice in their effect
And frame it for effect

Affect Effect
Big noses, wide smiles
Defects too
Stir the pot
Let it brew
Enjoy your communion with society's lot
For you will need some humour
Before you end up
In a grave plot.

Elephant ears

Christmas times

Magic in the air
It's Christmas in two days time
I give it a chance
Let it breathe through me

Some belief is good
Just let it run
A spirit circling the paddock
That flow, cooling the grass

I let it come
Just once a year
We all need it
To show humility, a way of being fair

It slides on
A few natural days
Savouring the light
Soft blue agapanthus
They sway just a bit
Putting the year to bed

A year stops
It pauses, holds still
We join together
We hope, we kiss
New minutes soon arrive
I look around
People in the dark
Feeling as one.

New trumpet

Golden trumpet
Alive in its case
Million notes unplayed

From Japan
Special
From Nanna
As an inheritance
From me
To John

Shiny buckles on its case
Clicking shut
Soft blue velvet
Keeping it so safe
Ready for a life of travel

It's got twirls
Three valves
Two tuning sleeves, I think
With gorgeous balance
Bright in your hands

Mad creativity ready to roll
Dark parties, flash nights
Sharp tunes, mellow moans
Sounds from the sea
Cries from the mountain
Await thee
Golden trumpet!

Joyful bauble

for Kristen Wischer

It's done
Christmas Day is over
It's wave on the beach
Come and gone
Leaving my toes cool
Gazing out to sea
Happily

Shall I tell you more?
More about what you know
You know it already
The way it can be
On your own day
In your own way

We all look to the sea
Answering its call
Long distance, short chirps
You know, the way water claps
Shell pieces
Catching the eye
Wet sand seeping back
Like a long sentence
The longer the better
As the tide comes in
Reaching further, with curves of wet
Decorating the beach

Christmas tree, Christmas tree
Growing further from where I stand
Ankle deep in the sand
Stealing me
A joyful bauble for the tree.

4. BROKEN GREY LEAD

Leucadendron

Bombed

You swooped twice
Once would have done
I felt fear
Your fearless attack
Such a sharp curve
My steps measured by you
I feel insulted and scared
Head down, elbows up
Fingers across my eyes
I cowered

Drunken focus

Mischievous alcoholic
Peers out the window
Surveys the scene
With a rosy gleam

Mind pickled in a vat
House neat, spare
No waste in sight
Tired jeans
Shirt three days old
If told

A miserable life
Tuned to perfection
Time allowed to pass
Waiting is a game
The game is to wait
And aim

Spring a trap
Buy a bottle
Unscrew its cap
Tilt or pour

Slip and slide
Careless, nothing to hide

The bliss arrives
With its own logic
Price paid, length of stone
Efficiency attained
Mischievous alcoholic.

2020

Glue the leaves back on the trees
Pack the soil around the trunk
Attach the poor birds
Whatever beautiful colour or type
Gently to the branches

The wind is fake
The sun won't shine
People have left
The gate won't swing
We live in a hollow clock

Our food is meagre
The cat is hungry
The children cry, mother is crying
Dad do something
Our times are darkening

Our house is clean
We wash ourselves, our clothes
Though soap is slim
Each day long
But we do little
The tough, pale light hurts

A baby dies
Grandparents go
There were no funerals
Just farewells in the mind
Our silent prayers floating up
Kind words, smiles, were said

We don't hope
That will not help

Better to be real
Stay close to your family
Remember your friends, talk to them
We all are living in the same hour

The rain will come
Traffic will thicken
Students and schools wake
Hold hands again
We stop and talk in the street, see a bird
Landing and hopping about
We move around her, watching her beak
Our children are sweeter
The wind blows, sun glows
The plague is drying up
Puddles of disease disappear

We will remember the year 2020
It taught us much
Those who called, those we trusted
Wives and husbands
Boys and girls
Cats and dogs
Back together.

Zoom funeral

Weird stuff
Jesus on a donkey
Someone put palm leaves out
Was that for the donkey?
Green colours on a gravure print
Jesus was brown
The air was bright
He was not quite riding
He was on, on the donkey
Not a cowboy for god
More of a cop
In a dress
On the Sunday School wall

Zoom funeral
I'm less confused now
Like cheap American TV
I'm there, apparently
On a screen
A box in the gloom
Some nice people
Seated around the coffin
There is a candle
They let me speak
Silver urn glistened

Show finished, off went the light
I felt dead too
The dead guy lived on
His own show!
Farewell, fare thee well
Brian dear
It was memorable
Scenic and emotional, dark

Joe Pascoe

Everyone had to behave
No sandwiches in shot
Zoom it did not

I think I would like a zoom funeral
A few camera angles
Or a Bertolucci sweep
A Fellini eccentric
The hypocritical relative

Interviewed for insights
Burn the inheritance
Before their eyes
Cash to ash
Don't ask, fuck you
Anger and love
Forever dancing
In sorrow

Who can act best?
Dress so well
Polish their shoes shiny
Control their faces, lipstick right
Have the best sad poem
A neat story, compassion-lite
I'm being too tough, wrong
My head feels off
The zoom funeral is cool
Not a poster at all
Stuck on a Sunday School wall
But a holy light pool
Atoms zapping bright.

Joe Pascoe

Half day

It's a day
Plain and not fancy
But it's a day
We try to be happy
Clowns in a pandemic
As slow as a rising circus tent
Putting it up with giant poles
Helped by the elephants
Tigers set free, softly growling around
Tricks of the mind
In such a slight way
On this day

I keep liking my pants
My clothes are generally cool
When you are locked down
Prisoners of time

You burrow in
Creep along the grain
Like beetles parting, forming a stream
On a day like today

A magpie has landed
Feeling fear

Seeing my eye
Plucked out from the sky
They use their beauty to deceive

The sounds sound stupid
A train toots, car tyres annoy
Human footsteps scrape to a stop
At the red letterbox
The big patterns are different
Together forming a wet brew in the rain

It arrived small, growing in mad stages
Matured as a mild threat
I am scared today of almost all
Colours on a shop
That someone will speak to me
Regarding some small offence
But the rain has now stopped
At midday.

Groove

It's Wednesday again
The days are spinning by
I'm learning to make them feel even
No wine at night
Coffee first thing in the morning
In between comes the day
Keeping reasonable to all
Some small surprises
But not many
If you watch out
They don't scare you

Today, a lamp fell on my head
That upset my wife
I was chased from the kitchen
But she made me a cup of tea
An odd exchange, but fair
That's a surprising surprise
Not significant, not predictable

I don't think it has occurred before
Maybe that's why I laughed
I don't always expect to laugh
Not these days at 64
Usually it's the universe
Not a lamp
That causes a giggle

My day is thus round
It arcs over
Graceful, suburban
In nice jumpers
Lucky me
Waiting for a safe shift

Another good meal
Timed chocolate treat
In the familiar supermarket

It's a mild life
Bordering on the fearful
Honest in a papery way
Keeping madness at bay
Has been my way
Yesterday and today
And I pray,
it stays that way
In my ironic groove.

Polite Melbourne

We are tired in the chemist shop
Standing equidistant
Not talking, responding flatly
Low cost version?
Waiting in the cool
Air-con and fans
TV struggling
We are tired
All of us
The staff, shoppers
Returning to normal
Pandemic easing
Easy acceptance
Queuing for health
Healthy queuing
Queuing for tiny pills
Pills in nice rows
Names called
Prescriptions filled
The new politeness.

Together

I remember their
Skulls
Shaped in my hands
As we kissed, made love

An oddness, perhaps
Handled in passion
Our fingers twisting
Lips meeting
The fine curves, backs of necks
Sweeps across the face
Cheek to cheek, when heaving
Feeling warm, panting

Voices
Moans
Little hellos, on the phone
How sweet to remember
The smiles and eyes
Amidst the perfumes
And clothes on the floor

Their cars, flats and cooking
Our lives shared for a while
Cupboard doors opened
Sometimes a pet, on the couch

Generous and incredible
Hands and all
Skin Bones
And walking

But the head
Framed by hair, framing love
It's impossible to forget

Humans and people
People and friends
Friends and you
Special you.

Pillar

Scattered

Even scattered has a feeling
Hold them close
Let them go

In your hand wrapped loose
Roll and flick
Land on the table
In the sand
Float for a moment
Dash like rain

A gambler tries it
Again and again
We do it
To let go some pain

Life can be too ordered
Avoid the pencil line
Draw in some clouds
Sunshine
Soil and even fame
Shake your chances
Risk it
Now!

Old crocodile

for Mark Cain

Do you need a long day?
To think things through
Measuring the past
Unmeasuring the future
Rationing your time
And your strength
What's left of it

Maybe you can't take a lot of pain
Not anymore
When you thought that was life
Normal almost
So it seemed
One thing shifted
And then another thing came

Now it's harder
Because you are softer
Giving in more easily
Wanting love
And lots of it
Not ever wishing to he alone
That eternal feeling
It went on and on
On bad Sunday afternoons

Some pain here and now
Or should I say
Here and then
It just comes sometimes
When it all seems wrong
You look for little hopes
A good haircut
Dollars in your pocket

Without a dream
Or destination
But at least a view
A chance again

That was youth
So many lucky days
Looking for pretty patterns
Unusual days
In many ways
Though sad is better than mad
I'm wildly past my use by date
I'm stuck together quite well
Being purposeful within myself
And for my family

It's a journey these days
A steady step is best
My health is my wealth
To be spent wisely
Slowly by prescription
Leave the bitterness alone
No arrogance needed anymore
Curb the rage though keep the anger
It adds colour
To the beige.

War's end

Plastic toy soldiers
Little men of war
Fitted with helmets and rifles
Small, even in a boy's hand
Cheaply green

Little bits of action
Rifles poised, standing and crouched
Two dozen maybe
Forming a haphazard line
Facing the matchsticks from my canon

No thought for much
Simple child's play
No sequence on display
Some sense of start and finish
From television, I guess

Meaning little but sparking anger
A necessary mind-state after school
The soldiers, not the teachers
Down low to the ground
Eyes level with theirs
Toppled and resurrected
Bunched in platoons for target practice

Nor did they surrender
Their brains were small
Packed away for another day
Fighting nowhere
No kisses farewell
No names or much known
War without purpose
Fought for mankind

Algorithms
High-level physics, computers
The game has changed
Gold braid swinging from shoulders
Military missions, coupled to what?
History will stop as drones advance
People are people in a war

It is over.

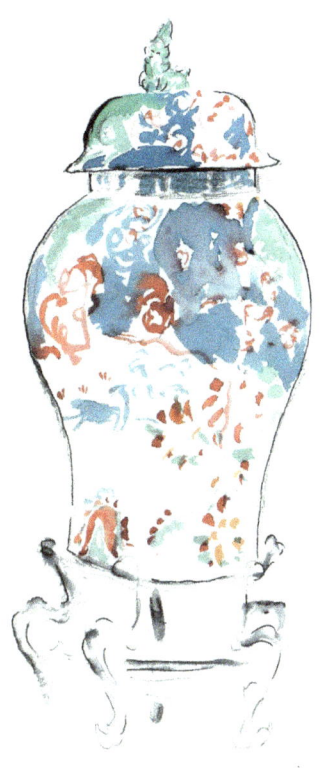

Vase at auction

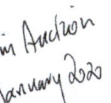

Amnesia

Forgetting
Fast
Almost unbelievable
So quick
We forgot

I'm happy to
It's slipping by
The plague
We do, must

Feeling lighter
Calves calming
Shoulders and forehead
Is everyone breathing out?
So lucky

A month or two
Then we get a jab
Vaccine
Easy waiting
Strange, the ordinariness
Our part of the world
Protected by Mother Earth's curve
Our oceans

Shall we forget more?
Those that died?
I felt nothing
Hardly a sneeze
Gone
Forgetting what?

Stendhal says goodbye

Stendhal stayed over
Red and black dressing gown
Warm in the corridor
He opened the door, a crack
Am I talking to him?
Or is he talking to me?
Did he wink?
Smiling and seeing me
Through two centuries past

Was that time was the same as this time?
But harder to explain
Wracked in all that historic pain
God was gone
Enlightened men went insane
Though satire though was the same
Churchmen, Lords and Ladies, Generals
Jolly uniforms, battles and guns

Literature was better
As the closer to mouths it came
Speaking as people
Lives felt through letters
Their moods on display
Moments caught array
Characters crushed by shot
Ports besieged, colourful flags fluttering
We marched, sailed and ran
As Stendahl
Stendhal dipped his pen

I listen in
As the tall clocks ticked
Wound firm by manners

Loves and vases of roses
In this manor house
What was your life like?
Did your adventure go on?
Surely you sometimes tripped
Like your characters do
As I remember reading you
Some pages of Red and Black
Searched anxiously for their promise
Before putting you back

Your hero falls and fate decides
Off with his head
The guillotine slides
Its downward smile
Sticky in the used basket
She kisses its forehead

But it was nice to see you at my door
But I think I shall roll over
And sleep some more
If you are still here
When I wake
I'll put on my slippers
Make some tea
And we can discuss
The nature of treachery

We can talk some more about war
Though where would your pen go
Without some red blood to flow?
Scratching on and on
We all need something to lean on
I'm worried now
Have you come to wish me well?
Has the Charon set off from the other shore,

dipping his oars
Rippling the black waters
Am I at death's door?
Is that why you come
With a wink to see my last blink
A story to live in,
you gave me that and more
With an arm artfully outstretched
I utter a blessing and mutter adieu!

5. PENCIL SHAVINGS

Butcher Bird 1

Old warbler

Just an old magpie
Left hanging around
Been in too many fights
To want any more
Singing for love
Singling for you
My warbling is true.

Ava

Which end to start with?
White paws
Tip of her flirty tail
Whiskers, smudgy nose?

Very still
Hiding in plain sight
Shaded under a bush

I have made a full study
Filled many notebooks
Discussed the matter

We feed her well
Science diet
Trips to the vet

Ava does not catch birds
Or preach about religion
Keeping her views to her self

Always strategic
And beautiful
Informing us on a need to know basis

We pat her
Make way
Greet her each day
And love her just so.

The trees are talking to me

The trees are talking to me
Judges in the landscape
Limbs pointing out
Gatherers of evidence
Leaves recording thoughts
Their contents secret
Measuring gold and pollution
Great hairy trunks as tough as fibre can be
Blotched with convincing colours
True witnesses to Australian history
They judge us for the black man

We composted their culture
Became fertilised by their art
Saving our concrete world from sinking
These trees are older than us
And may stay longer than our white nation
It's possible you know
That's what they say.

Sherbrooke forest

I hear you calling back
A coo-eee on the forest track
Not at all lost
Just friendly
You are in your coat
Furry hat
You might get mistaken
By a friendly bat

It's a beautiful day
The trees seem very tall
And it's damp on the forest floor
Dizzy high-rise above
Squirming world below

There's that whooping sound
A crack
Always together
Whoop, crack
I hurry on
And see your hat.

Paddock

Barbed wire
What's over there?
Silent echoes.

Brave

Tough sculpture park
Steel baking in the sun
Me wandering around
Feet brushing the dry grass
Water birds by the mossy lake
Noisy and well feed

Warm wind blows
This army will stand still
A concrete acropolis
Down Frankston way

The invisible battle
Australia's civil war
Those that know art
In perpetual formation
Their enemies will not be befriended
Or laid siege
By so many sculptures

But we walk around
Hearing their sound
Trials and triumphs
Commissions and commuters
Defending the museum

As clouds pass
And people go
In silent sentinel
Brave Sculpture Park.

Night time radio

for Cahaya Fuller

Listening to the radio
At night
Airwaves bright
Undeniably near
Close by my ear
Wrapped in bed
Blankets of sound
Snug all around

Sunday music
Able to be taken in
Luxury
In the dark air
Made for this occasion

Rather timeless
But not loosely so
A finite precision
In tune
Clear as a bell
Whether in the lonely country
Or city-like alert
Healing and mending
The sun gone
No need to fret
The day is done
Let sleep approach
Your mind wander undone

Beautiful song and ample tones
Metronome ticks
Heart beats
Could be Elvis
An orchestra that speaks

Night's curtain rises
Another performance
The stage is set
New dreams
New hopes
Cast their coloured lights
Rich red

Fern gully green
Gold sparkles
In the stream
As you dream

Listening to the radio
At night
Airwaves bright
Undeniably intimate
Close by my ear
Wrapped in bed
Blankets of sound
Snug all around.

Astra concert in real time

vale John Nixon

I feel
Tormented within the space
Sound coaxing relaxation
Toward a slow end
We go there in our rows
Hundreds of us in fear

Guarded by the priests
Acting like sparrows
Pecking at our minds
Dissolving in the organ music
Sopranos squeak
Off-piste with their lyrics
Snatches of impatient narratives
Revolving over and over
Marrying us in heaven
And somewhere else
A personal ledge

The short pipes pop
The chorus takes off again
Rollicking on the high seas
Drowning in the bass scrum
Humane and human

Paper shuffled for another carol
In clever announcement
Choir unsparingly bouncing back
A concert for the ready
Those that know the score
With mild fury
And thumping complexity
Shifting forward as a mass of one
Discordant and witty

We now rest in a humming movement
Still the hypnotic zing
Floats us on
Inviting us to swim
Blessed in the cool ocean.

Didge

for Eric Brown

Didge
Growling, moaning
For the earth
For the birds
So tough, sweet too
Telling and talking
Warming all around
In the room

Didge
We stand, you sit
Growling on
Floating around
Cooking the vibe
Our song, coming in
Flying and hunting
Making truth

Black man, leader
Champion
Crowning the land
Bringing it to life
Birthing ancient time
Wavering and beating time
Beautiful and strong
Calling the mob to love
Airwaves shimmering
Speaking
The talk
Talking to you.

6. DOTS

Daphne wreath

Outside the alphabet

for Andy Fuller

Taking siege outside the alphabet
Watching for letters, ready to run
Lure set, chocolate on a string
Throw it in
Tug it back
To complete the trap

Camped outside the walls
Tall letters, fat ones
i's missing their dots
Dots chasing i's
Falling into ditches
Bouncing bare

Need more letters, hundreds
The whole castle
Knights, ladies and children
I promise to look after you
Come join my poem
See what you can do
Lots of lovely chocolate
No strings attached
Waiting here for you.

Homage to metrical poetry

for Robert Nelson

Dance words dance
On the page
Off the page
Off and of, let's dance
Together, you lead, I'll follow
See how stylish you can be
But come back for me
I like your colours and zest
Quick, cheat
Laugh along the way
I'll let you do what you like
Chasing the sun
Hoping fun, sideways glance
Beware the shadows don't get deep
Dance little words
The ands and buts
It, to, a, thought
Tiny cushions, set the pace
Count you up
Make metric feet
Add a letter, become bigger
Hippopotamus, elevated
Very hippo-like
I like
I like
I like
To help the hippopotamus dance.

Dice

Every dice thrower has an action
A lucky flick
Hopeful glance
Rattle and roll

Stops and looks back
Those dice do
How do you do?

They say
You look
Lucky or not
Pleasure and gain
Loss, something to explain

Warmer dice
Cold stones
Men's looks
Whisky talking
Foolish grins
Nonchalant farts

Hand them in, I'm done
No more fun, they won
One more go, before I go
Double sixes, snake eyes
Look to the skies
Blow on my hand
Rattle them clean
Lose the bad luck
Fuck it, I'm not coming back!

David

for Prof David Jamieson

Maths tumbling around
Spiralling, fast
Twisting
Within a million atoms
Floating in and out of order
Simultaneous flipping, changing places
Changing maths
Inside out, elsewhere too
Calculating the infinite

I tried to understand
Quantum computing
This exploration into reality
Now squiggles on a small whiteboard
Textas on smudged vinyl
What? I asked

Never to know
Able to respect
One day to fear
Or pray

The future
In several places at once
Who will own it?
Its purpose?
Answers, control
New questions
Life and maths together
In harmony.

Ivanhoe maple tree

for Don Walters

Pink blossom tree
Doted flowers in the rain
Japanese maple skin
Polished and hard
Traffic light flicks
Pedestrian signal beeps

Nestled against a wall
A white funeral parlour
Nicely trimmed
Fitting well, snuggled in
Dozens of years old
Caught in a gentle fold
Near the footpath
Near life

You are not a message
Not an omen
Planted too close
Never to spread out
A third cropped
Your branches half radiant

Japanese split leaf maple
Protected from the north winds
Safe from the western sun
You will never see it set
As you wave to the post office

We must all get on
Restaurant, supermarket
Pensioners soon to fill their caskets
School boys laugh and run
Traffic, prams rolling by

Blossoms ready to fly
This corner of a round world
It won't much change
Small clots of people
Poodle blends on leads
An even mingling of tones
Everyone mostly half busy
Receding from the partial tree
Still very pretty
Especially if you are a bee.

Kim

for Kim Guttridge

Perched on a stool next to friend Kim
A good long day
Concluding with a meal
At Tiamo's on Lygon Street

First we went up bush
To connect with the printed soul
Known as George Baldessin
Watched by his widow
She deals with history
The long shadow of fame and death

A strong woman
Lean like the trees
Marks in the bush
As we had coffee and talked

Her gaze was one I had felt before
Carrying a flame
With all its pain and form
Galvanised in art

From there to Eltham
More ruggedness at Montsalvat
A different proposition
Of medieval might
And a community of artists
Self-conscious in its vision

On we went
A book launch
A great book on the Mallee
Four historians
Exploring an Australian underbelly

Great levelling dirt
With almost nothing to say
Powerful in its way
Landscape and ecology
Roots and fine dust
Somehow this land sits across Australia
Not nothing but opaque

We sit now in Tiamo
Enjoying the Italian girls
Performing to our eating
A superb play
They are doing a dance
Around the pay point
A lure linking customer and food
A feeling we have experienced all day

We share with them
Our gaze, our appreciation
For their culture
And how it plays
On this long, fun Saturday.

Funky specs

On a rock

My timing was off
It's critical with teenagers
How about this for a book title?
I said
Thinking of something

Eve dived sideways
The couch is springy
As was her reply
Uttered to her iPhone
'On a rock'

I still laugh
An inward giggle
Next day and the next

The poetry world
If I was so game
Hard to imagine
Or explain
A plop on a boulder
In bronze
Photographed well
At dawn

Keep your freedom Evie
It's a wonderful thing
No malice intended
Nor offence taken
Some posh words would be good
But nothing seems
To rhyme right
With on a rock
Except my happy memory
Of the funny shock.

Hard to title

for Ro Doolan

It's frightening
How much of the past we can see
Candle flickering
Walking down the corridor
In silence
Head beating
Full

It seemed important
But no more
Returning and looking
Feeling
Almost tasting
Turning the key
Doors acting as ghosts
Moving

Visit for a short while
Leave as you came
Fold the memories neatly
Buttons astray
Mess

Those shadows grow larger
In the past
It's a mistake
But it's a truth
Remember as you do
To gain a foothold
Back
Dream forward
Dare it
Keep it quiet
But dream on

Joe Pascoe

Dare to see
Be there
In the future

From here you can see
Across the land
By the beach
To hear the waves
Beating
Like a heart.

Rusting

Black sandpaper rubbing at reality
Like a million stars those bumps
Smoothing back the folds of time
In my hand back and forth
No task, just a memory
Drawn from inside
Returning to my hand
To recall a wider context
Underneath the house
Engaged in a private project
Something requiring shining
A metal surface a part of some thing
To be restored
Rescued from rust
A childhood object needing alchemy
It's gone now
Except the action
And the place
Lodged in my mind
Between two flakes of time
Or rust.

Circle

Standing in a circle
Stretching around, horizon to horizon
Nearby hill, tapering to rocks
Running out to sea
To Wilson's Promontory
Anti-clockwise
Wrapping Waratah Bay
How far across?
15 kilometres I say

Feeling irritated, merely mildly
Sunlight lifting the sand
Grey to soft yellow
Some waves crinkling, distant surf

Rock pools forming Galápagos Islands
Dramatic in miniature
Questionable and ugly on mass
Lava flows angling to the water
Sizzling into rectangles

Strewn with seaweed, readying for night's dance
My wife is collecting shells
Small cowries with brown backs

I can't quite measure my words
Or name all the elements
And blend them right
Where to place the caravan park?
Happy dogs, young families?
Here in the middle of life.

Torquay sunrise

for John O'Neil

John
High on the sands
In the dark
Sunrise to come

Around us is the kelp
Disguised calligraphy
The ocean talks
Expressive in soft bronze
Wet, strewn, blown

His long strides roll
Waves seep in
The new dawn opens
Speaking quietly at first

Slowly mouthing its omen
I give you a new day
Which he takes, turning

Marmalade sky
Running with butter
Flowing generously
Stars gone, Moon out
A silver memory on the wet sheen

It's a fine sunrise
Perfect at Torquay
Not discussed, just loved
Blessing the beach
Photographed in the mind
Tall John
Happy John
Stored in the cloud
Private

Its coffee
Mud rich
Its ducks
Circling baby Finn
And Peg, always present
Children three
Jewels on his windswept tree.

Little fishes

We are in a fish bowl
Peering out through the glass
Tinkle and bubbles above the rubble
Gliding down and curving
In the quiet
We flick left and right
On our flight

I see the room
Magnified and silent
Our glass is clean
The waiting room is full
We have a job to do
Dancing in the sun
Cheering everyone

They watch our bonsai world and tap hello
It's where we are in the evolutionary scale
Away from germs and sorrows within ourselves
Pairing and eating for a while

Down to the sunken treasure
Up to the popping top
Between the plastic grass
Suspended in something like a dream
That little boy likes us
His thumb is sore

The old lady is coughing
Soon for a wooden coffin
We will try harder for her
A lifetime of helping on her face
We keep moving
Swimming is our joy

Toward evening we slow to feed
As the kind receptionist
Turns off the light
And she says, 'Good night'.

7. Last Pages

Palm

Last dream

She lay as a tree might
A fallen branch
Well shaped
In line with the hill
My privilege to watch
A son in attendance
I would never had known
Could never had understood

There was a simple dignity
Body straight and mouth open
An impressive ending
No anguish or pain
Wearing down to a perfect silence

It was quiet
She was quiet
I was without tears
No final howl by anyone
It was an event
Almost without punctuation
Poem-like

The only angle was me to her
Chair and bed in a polite arrangement
A decent room

Yes I had packed everything
Ready to break camp at dawn
Or whenever
With our customary order
Known to all hikers
You do it to not forget
To be ready

I was searching too
Not for gold
I wanted to ease meaning from the hospital room
But like a fish tank
Its sides were touchable
Even the corners
I looked everywhere, finding little
I think the talismans were basic
Functional yet vague
Such is dementia
My eyes failed
And yet her clothes spoke
Pretty flowers and happier cottons
This country girl

The time came
We drove home with her items
Not knowing much more about her
Except her dreams of a softer life
With gardens and a cottage
Where people talked in the streets
Air warmed by the sun
And friendly dogs and kids ran.

So simple

3.04
An extra stillness
I looked
No breathing
Ah but she might again
I was not sure
3.05 check the time carefully
Why?
To try and be certain
To measure life
And be able to tell others
Unrelatedly I went to her toilet
To use a little time
And be ready when many people would come
Ailsa was very still, still

My fingers
The back of them
Brushed her checks
As you should with lavenders flowers
To not bruise
A coldness
Confirmation

I pressed the nurse's button
Gathered in a worker from the corridor
'Is she dead?'
A look
An internal call
A nurse
'Sorry for your loss'
Dead was not said
Blabbed the facts to Bob
'I will come back!'

Joe Pascoe

An ethereal state
Which I liked
Followed
It felt red
No other word
Red
In its meaning of dominant and real
Of toys even
It is how it has always made me feel

For a good while
Sorry for you loss
Said

Mother became cold
A personal prayer
Whatever it is you do
Talking in the corridor
We sit together
Lyndel, Steve, Bob and me
A good conversation
Confirmation of details
3.05 was the deal

Cup of tea and biscuits
Staff were kind
Shocked too
Ailsa was strong
And a long time care
We thanked them
I went to say a final 'bye'
A warning look from a nurse
I soon understood why
Death is hard
It stiffens the face
In her case

No gentle halo
An El Greco grimace instead
Painted in wasted pink
Stretched out
Skull and skin
Fixed ahead

A tough goodbye
To be remembered until I die
So that is death
It really is dead
Her life-tree was dry
From her own long goodbye

In gratitude now
The breathe gone
A love lingered in the room
Even though she had gone
Lyndel and I went home

Told our children Eve and John
'She loved you'
Her soft kitten and small bear
Under the Christmas tree
Smile with us you lovely things!

Mother dear,
Be our friend in the open sky
Speak sometimes as you will
This time I might stand still!

Innocent snow

Silent snow
Outside the car window
Looking into a hill
Almost flat up
Spindly gums dripping out

Leaves hanging, free and grey
White land, black road
Moist as the car revs mildly
Snicking through its gears
We are snug

People and jumpers
Coats rolled up
Bags and gloves
Everything warm, wary
Its cold outside

More corners
Climbing, penetrating
Mystery unfolding, another land

Great car parks, messy mud, buses
Fumes and fog
Cheerful I think
I bunk in, learn to ski
Remembering the best
Flight, white
Soundless again
Careful judgements, hot chocolates
Fitting in
Mechanical lifts, great wheels
Learning more
Snow, in it

Laughing
Swivel, stand up
Getting better, like something
A giraffe, a baby
Innocent.

Burnt forest

Redemption
Punishment
Black trees, grass gone
Nowhere to walk
Or run, forest animals
But do we hear you?

You roared
We screamed
But did not understand

Softened soot
Charming underneath
Puffs of ash
Bark marking our clothes
We move through

The light is subdued
Nothing glistens
Don't say it is beautiful, not yet
Today it is in prayer
Offering little comfort

Walk further
Feel lost
Lose track of space
Change your view
Stop, breath
Try not to think
Meditate
Let thoughts come
Hear the peace
Be blind.

Joe Pascoe

Three old men

Three old men
Bend their voices
Recalling the past
Strumming the present
To find a song for today

At lunch
Three round pizzas
Ascending in complexity
Three deserts
Descending in size

We balance our lives
Knowing our wives
Seeing the magic in our children
Their freedoms, stories anew
Our love

A circuit of conversation
Rolling around
Pushed like a playground swing
Higher and higher
We see the sky
Glimpsing fancy clouds
The sunbeams of youth
Showing through

We have survived, growing
Plants in our garden
Plots tendered
Seeds placed
Our soil, our life
A fine lunch.

Bouquet

Columbarium

I'm back mother
I've come to visit you
In your place in the memorial wall
Up here in Shepparton town

You liked Shepparton
You found the people easy
Friendly and helpful
Ask a question
Get a nice answer
It surprised you

I liked it too
Never felt reproached
As I worked

You are together with Ian
Racing cars and happy times
It's vivid for me
Tears soften my eyes

I'm hard
But going rusty, mellow
Reviewing and believing you
As I go along, writing poems
Hoping, struggling too
Without you

That's life, death
After the death
The dead stay dead
It's hard to visit you in the wall
...
Two hot donuts

Free with your coffee
Laminex tables, cinnamon smiles
Tasty cafe
Shepparton town

I've come to visit mum
She is in the memorial wall
It's made the whole town a memory
A floating cloud
Where people talk and cars go by

Humble in my pride
Flat land, one sand hill
Lunette type, ancient
Upon which the Columbian sits

People ask why
I tell them
'She was a country girl
Rockhampton is too far away'
Quiet by the river
Ailsa and Ian will stay

...

We visited mum's grave
It went well
Our first visit together
All together

A noble cemetery
Built with history
History built it
In this old town
Like a rock rounded
It feels outdoors

Somehow gathering a light breeze
Or breezes of light
Such is the ambiguity
Of life in death

You think, you hope
For a communication
But it can't happen
You may speak, yes
But your answer won't reveal
It's not a telephone exchange, this cemetery

I am new to this business
But I like the Columbarium
The niche, which I kissed
And turned away

Time will pass
For me, not them
Fine filaments of memory
An emotional lava
Cooling and winding
Winding then cooling
In me

A message did come, later
A reflection of the day
'Don't give up', it said
That's OK
Softly.

Bits of time
for Carla Pascoe Leahy

It's those bits of your life
Stairs, a footpath
Nonchalant

Resting places for your memories
Boring and in between
With hardly a conversation
Nothing

A mile on a highway
There was a tree
That curve

Car positioned for speed
Seeking the apex
Gliding through

Not intended for contemplation
Years in an office
Elevator buttons

Like shoelaces
Keeping things together
Time, tasks

Barbed wire or string
Fencing you in
No choice, pay day

Walking from the station
Or to the station
Short minutes
So well recalled
Your state of mind
Jungle thick, dense

Epilogue

Lemon scented gum 2

Great Mountain

for Anthony Pearse

Warmth in the words
To set a fire
Ease the cold thoughts away

Scoop some leaves
In search of twigs
Fine, ready to burn
Turning my back to the wind

Water from the river
Food from the pack
Evening from the long walk

Backpack against a tree
Light tent stretched quite tight
All organised in the lengthening night

In those days I slept
Picking my ground
Falling deep down, clear and sound

Miles and miles away
Usually a bit lost
Strange to think that way

Not needing a lot
But very persistent, billy boiling hot
In nature, on a map

Not foolish with energy
Taking diagonals, curving over the land
Avoiding gullies, hearing streams
Shoelaces firm, hat on
Trudging up slopes
Blisters may wince, shoulders sometimes ache

Further along, loose stones at the top
Those last few hundred yards
Harking loneliness, cooler winds
Lifting horizon, longer strides
Weight dropping off, a victory in sight

Casting around the giant land
Genuine awe held in its hand
Great Mount Terrible
Named for its brutal height
And watchtower, for scanning for fires alight

We felt no fear
An easy feeling, descending after a while
A bit more lost, that's true
Headed downhill, tracking north
Finding the bitumen road at Ten Mile

The Woods Point Road is long
It had to swerve and snake around
I think it was there because it had to be
People looking for gold you see
We found heat, and the top
We found what we got
A good look, a good friend
A journey shared
To the end.

Unring that bell song
for Norman Rosenblatt

You can't
Can't
Can't unring that bell

Change the church spire
Change the land
Look the other way

But still
Still
Still can't unring that bell

You said it
I said it too
Thunder rolling

Dark clouds
Clouds and heavy rain
Soaking us through

Ring that bell
Hope that it chimes
Rings true

Got to love you
Hold true
Wet rope slipping through

Ring those bells
Make them sing
Forget everything

A new song
Singing
Ringing
Thinking
Listening too

Ring those bells
Can't be unrung
Sing, sing.

About

Joe Pascoe

Joe Pascoe (b. 1956) lives in Ivanhoe, Melbourne, Australia. He had a long career in the visual arts including roles at Geelong Art Gallery, Victoria Ministry for the Arts, Shepparton Art Gallery, Australia Council for the Arts and Craft Victoria. The poem Museum boy tells of his earliest interest in museums and libraries.

Joe's other books of poetry are *Gum Tree Burning* (2019) and *Frangipani* (2020) Reading Sideways Press. *Sharp Pencil* completes a loose story arc that weaves through to suggest a love of observation.

Sam Golding

Sam Golding (b. 1964) lives in Camberwell, Melbourne, Australia. Sam is a lawyer and artist with an extensive exhibition history. The artworks in *Sharp Pencil* featured in an exhibition of the same name, at the Malvern Artists Society in 2021.

You enter Sam's artwork through the alacrity of his stroke, his hand, his presence, which invite you to share in a moment. It could be a bird or a waving branch, maybe a seascape, but the solution he gives to the question of looking, is always offered with warmth and
beauty. *Sharp Pencil* as an exhibition shares a love of contemplation with this book of poems. Sight and imagination come together in both art forms, with space for the viewer or reader to live in a fresh moment again.

www.ingramcontent.com/pod-product-compliance
Lightning Source LLC
Chambersburg PA
CBHW070255010526
44107CB00056B/2473